Careers in Computer Science

ReferencePoint Press®

Other titles in the *Exploring Careers* series include:

Careers in Business Administration
Careers in Digital Media
Careers in Entertainment
Careers in Environmental Conservation
Careers in Medicine

EXPLORING
CAREERS

Careers in Computer Science

Carla Mooney

ReferencePoint
Press®

© 2018 ReferencePoint Press, Inc.
Printed in the United States

For more information, contact:
ReferencePoint Press, Inc.
PO Box 27779
San Diego, CA 92198
www.ReferencePointPress.com

LIBRARY OF CONGRESS CATALOGING-IN-PUBLICATION DATA

Name: Mooney, Carla, 1970– author.
Title: Careers in Computer Science/by Carla Mooney.
Description: San Diego, CA: ReferencePoint Press, Inc., 2018. | Series: Exploring careers series | Includes bibliographical references and index. | Audience: Grades 9 to 12.
Identifiers: LCCN 2017009897 (print) | LCCN 2017013012 (ebook) | ISBN 9781682821954 (eBook) | ISBN 9781682821947 (hardback)
Subjects: LCSH: Computer science—Juvenile literature.
Classification: LCC QA76.25 (ebook) | LCC QA76.25 .M66 2018 (print) | DDC 004--dc23
LC record available at https://lccn.loc.gov/2017009897

Contents

Searching for System Weaknesses

Aleksander Gorkowienko is a principal consultant at 7Safe, a penetration testing company. He spends most of his day trying to break into companies' computer systems. One of the many careers in computer science, penetration testing is the practice of testing a computer system, web application, or network to find security weaknesses. In his job, Gorkowienko uses real-world criminal hacking techniques to try to find weaknesses in a client's systems and procedures. While each client is different, the goal is the same: to simulate the attacks that real-world criminal hackers launch daily and report their success or failure to the client.

For Gorkowienko, every client presents a unique challenge. He encounters different technologies for each job, from modern web apps to outdated computer systems. Sometimes he performs a Structured Query Language injection, in which he places a query into a database that allows him to maliciously manipulate the database. Other times he carries out a phishing attack, in which he impersonates someone over the phone or via e-mail to get security information such as a password. Regardless of which technique he uses, the main goal is to detect weaknesses in the client's systems to prevent data breaches and loss. "It's [about] prevention, rather than trying to stop the fire when it's already too late," he says in an April 2016 article for *Computerworld UK*.

For one client, Gorkowienko and his team of penetration testers made a copy of the client's website. They then created a form and sent out official-looking e-mails that were designed to trick the client's employees into disclosing sensitive information. "One of the people on the target list was a guy—he was the only one in the company responsible for the maintenance of this website," Gorkowienko says.

"Only he had access to it. He saw the email, clicked the link, filled in the form, pressed the submit button—only afterwards did he ask himself: 'Who the hell created the form?'" By showing the employee his mistake, Gorkowienko's team was able to help him and the client understand where they needed more security training.

What Is Computer Science?

Computer science is a wide career field that includes many positions, from penetration tester to software developer to security analyst. Computer science professionals are responsible for an organization's computer hardware, networks, and software systems. They work for companies in almost every industry, including health care, services, manufacturing, nonprofit, finance, technology, retail, government, and more. They design, create, and invent new technology and find new uses for existing technology. They spend their days solving complex technology problems and ensuring that an organization's computer systems and networks run smoothly and securely.

Knowing how to code is just one aspect of computer science. Professionals in this field also study how computer equipment and software perform. They design easy-to-use applications that operate on a variety of devices, from laptops to mobile phones.

Computer science professionals work in a wide range of careers. They might be involved with computer hardware architecture, in which they discover new ways for computers to process information. They might use new materials and techniques to design computer processors that work faster and more powerfully. Other computer scientists might work on developing virtual reality technology, which makes video game users feel as if they are inside the game. Still others support users across an organization, answering questions and solving technology problems.

A Growing Demand

According to the Bureau of Labor Statistics, the demand for computer and information technology professionals is expected to grow 12 percent between 2014 and 2024, which is faster than the average

Careers in Computer Science

Occupation	Minimal Education Requirements	2015 Median Salary
Computer and information systems manager	Bachelor's degree	$131,600
Computer hardware engineer	Bachelor's degree	$111,730
Computer network architect	Bachelor's degree	$100,240
Computer programmer	Bachelor's degree	$79,530
Computer support specialist	Associate's degree	$51,470
Computer systems analyst	Bachelor's degree	$85,800
Information security analyst	Bachelor's degree	$90,120
Network and computer systems administrator	Bachelor's degree	$77,810
Software developer	Bachelor's degree	$100,690
Technical writer	Bachelor's degree	$70,240
Web developer	Associate's degree	$64,970

Source: Bureau of Labor Statistics, *Occupational Outlook Handbook*, 2016. www.bls.gov.

rate for all occupations. Most computer science careers require students to earn a bachelor's or master's degree from a four-year college or university, while a few careers require just an associate's degree or related work experience.

Students interested in this field can major in computer science, information systems, computer engineering, or a related area. Often students take a wide variety of computer science classes, such as programming languages, network architecture, database design, engineering, and mathematics. Many also concentrate in specific areas, such as software engineering, computer systems and networks, data science, artificial intelligence, and security. Across all concentrations, a degree in computer science provides a foundation of technical skills that can be used in a wide range of technology-related careers.

Software Developer

People use computers, smartphones, tablets, and other technological devices every day, and sometimes all at once. Software developers create the programs that run these devices. Some software developers create applications that allow users to do a specific task on a computer or device. Others create the underlying systems that allow a device to operate or control a network.

When working on a new software program, developers often start by talking to the client or other employees about how they plan to use the software. From these discussions, the developer determines the most important functions that users want to see included. Developers also determine other requirements, such as security and performance needs. With these in mind, software developers design the program. Then they hand the design off to computer programmers, who write and test the program's code, which tells the program what to do and how to perform. Software developers typically work very closely with computer programmers when writing the program's

At a Glance

Software Developer

Minimum Educational Requirements
Bachelor's degree

Personal Qualities
Strong analytical, computer, and communication skills

Certification and Licensing
Not required, but can strengthen résumé

Working Conditions
Office environment

Salary Range
Median pay of $100,690 in 2015

Number of Jobs
About 1.1 million as of 2014

Future Job Outlook
Projected growth of 17 percent through 2024

Software developers confer on a new program. These tech professionals create the programs that run the computers, smartphones, tablets, and other devices that people use every day.

code, answering any questions that may arise. In some companies, software developers write the code themselves.

If a program does not work as expected, software developers tweak the design to fix any bugs, errors, or other problems. Even after a program is released to users, software developers may have to tinker with the design later, to upgrade the program and maintain it.

Some software developers are called applications software developers because they develop computer applications. Some design commercial software for general users, such as TurboTax or Photoshop. Others design custom software for specific users, such as inventory tracking software (which manufacturers use). Still others create complex databases for companies, while some create software that can be used over the Internet.

Other software developers work on the systems that run computers and networks. They are called systems software developers. They work to create the operating systems that come with every new computer, such as Microsoft Windows, macOS, and Linux. Others develop operating systems for other types of electronic equipment, such as smartphones or new cars. Some systems software designers build custom systems for specific companies. Systems software designers often create system interfaces such as a graphical user interface. These programs allow users to interact with computers.

Claire Lock is a software developer for Riverview Law, a United Kingdom–based legal services firm. In her role, Lock's typical day depends on what her current project is. "The type of work I undertake on any given day will differ depending on what stage a project is currently at," she says in an April 2014 interview posted on the Totaljobs website. At the beginning of a new project, Lock may be involved in talking to users about what they need the software to accomplish. Then she might work on developing and implementing the new software. Once a prototype is completed, she will test the software and document her findings. "This keeps the job interesting because the nature of the work changes as a project progresses," she says. Lock says that the types of projects that come across her desk are always changing. "The best thing about my job is the variety," she explains. "One day I may be attending requirement meetings, the next I'll be coding a custom workflow and the day after that I may be writing a report. This helps to keep things fresh and interesting." Lock says the most satisfying parts of her job include problem solving and coming up with solutions to complicated situations.

How Do You Become Software Developer?

Education

Most software developers have a bachelor's degree in computer science, software engineering, or a related field. For some positions, a degree in mathematics is acceptable. Generally, students take courses in computer programming, operating systems, and networks. Many also take math classes like calculus, differential equations, and linear algebra. In some degree programs, students complete a senior design project that allows them to apply what they have learned.

Certification and Licensing

Although this field has no required certifications or licenses, getting certified can improve your chance of landing a job. John Reed is a senior executive director at Robert Half Technology, a staffing firm that specializes in information technology jobs. He says that many employers regard certifications as proof that a candidate has technical skills in specific areas of programming or development. "Certifications may be seen as a key differentiator for candidates seeking roles on technology teams," says Reed in an August 2015 interview on the *InfoWorld* website.

Many organizations offer certifications that can strengthen a candidate's résumé. For example, developers can earn an entry-level Microsoft Technology Associate Developer certification and several intermediate-level Microsoft Certified Solutions Developer certifications.

Volunteer Work and Internships

Many students interested in working as a software developer gain experience by doing an internship while in college. While a computer science student at Ohio State University, Dalton Flanagan held a summer internship at the investment bank JPMorgan Chase. Flanagan worked as an application developer intern on a team of software developers. He wrote code to support one of the bank's many computer applications. Flanagan says the experience was extremely valuable. "As you can imagine, writing software in a classroom is much different than writing software in the 'real world,'" he said in a November 2015 interview posted on the university's website. "My internship provided me with a perspective of how industry differs from the classroom."

Flanagan believes that his internship will give him an advantage when searching for a job after graduation. "Professionally, I have a major advantage with an internship under my belt," he says. "Industry experience is sometimes considered as important as GPA when applying to jobs, and full-time candidates with prior internship experiences have much more success in the post-graduation job search than those who do not."

Skills and Personality

Successful software developers need solid problem-solving, analytical, computer, and communication skills. They need to possess both creativity and technical skills if they are to turn their ideas into working programs. Developers also communicate with many people in an organization, from other computer programmers to managers, who may be less familiar with technical concepts. They must therefore be able to give clear instructions to coworkers and explain to users how software works. Therefore, software developers must have strong communication skills.

It is also important for software developers to have solid time-management skills and to pay attention to detail. They frequently work on several parts of an application or system at once, which means they must be very organized and efficient. Software developers should also have some knowledge of the industry in which they work. For example, developers who work for a clothing retailer should know about the retail industry so they can design the most effective software.

On the Job

Employers and Working Conditions

Many software developers work for software publishers or companies that specialize in computer systems and services. Some work for computer or other electronics manufacturers. According to the Bureau of Labor Statistics (BLS), the industries that employed the most software developers in 2014 were computer systems design and related services (33 percent), software publishers (8 percent), finance and insurance (8 percent), and computer and electronic product manufacturing (8 percent).

Regardless of industry, software developers spend most of their time working in an office. Some telecommute and work from home or another location outside the office. No matter where they work, they spend a lot of time in front of a computer. Most software developers work full time (40 hours per week). According to the BLS, long hours are common.

Iliya Koreschev is a senior software engineer at video game developer Zynga. Sometimes he has to stay up all night to finish a project on time. Other times he has to work the entire weekend, canceling other planned activities to work. Koreschev says this is more common in start-up companies because there are fewer developers to share the work and less time to complete a project.

Although this industry has historically been dominated by men, the number of female software developers is growing. According to a 2015 Evans Data survey, 22.2 percent of software developers in 2015 were female, the highest number in the past fifteen years. "The population of female software developers has been steadily growing since the last recession," says Janel Garvin, chief executive officer of Evans Data, in an April 2015 article published on the *eWeek* website. "Women are starting to view technology as a profession with a very favorable future and are beginning to believe it's a world that's accessible to them."

Earnings

According to the BLS, as of May 2015 the median annual pay for software developers was $100,690. The median pay for systems software developers ($105,570) was slightly higher than the median pay for applications developers ($98,260). Software developers typically receive other benefits too, which can be worth thousands of dollars. Benefits vary from employer to employer but usually include paid vacation and sick leave, bonuses, medical and dental insurance, education or tuition reimbursement benefits, retirement benefits, and life insurance.

Opportunities for Advancement

Software developers can advance to become information technology (IT) project managers. In this position, they typically supervise a software project from planning through implementation. They oversee a team of software developers and monitor progress to make sure the project meets deadlines, incorporates all requirements, and stays within its budget.

What Is the Future Outlook for Software Developers?

The job outlook for software developers is very good. According to the BLS's *Occupational Outlook Handbook*, employment of developers is projected to grow 17 percent from 2014 to 2024. This growth rate is much faster than the average rate for all occupations.

The main driver of such rapid growth in this field is the increase in demand for computer software. One area of growth will come from the Internet of Things, which connects everyday devices such as watches, appliances, heating and cooling units, and self-driving cars to the Internet. Software developers will be needed to write the programs that run these devices, as well as the programs that connect them to the Internet. Also, all of these devices will need to work together, making developers with experience in developing interfaces to connect devices across different platforms and gateways in high demand.

An increased focus on computer and network security may also result in more demand for security software. Hacking attacks are growing, and their cost to organizations is increasing. According to the Ponemon Institute's *2015 Cost of Cyber Crime* report, companies reported an average of 160 successful cyberattacks each week. Of the companies surveyed, these attacks cost between $1.9 million to $65 million in 2015. Therefore, developers will be needed to create software that protects computer networks and infrastructure.

Because software developer jobs pay well, competition for these jobs is strong. Candidates who have the most up-to-date programming languages and computer skills will have the best prospects for landing a job.

Find Out More

Association of Software Professionals (ASP)
PO Box 1522
Martinsville, IN 46151
website: http://asp-software.org

The ASP is a professional trade association of software developers who are creating and marketing leading-edge applications. It offers several resources, including a monthly newsletter, numerous articles, and forums for member discussions.

CompTIA
3500 Lacey Rd., Suite 100
Downers Grove, IL 60515
website: www.comptia.org

CompTIA provides many IT certifications and education resources for professionals in information technology, including software developers. The organization also advocates for the IT industry at the local, state, and federal government levels.

IEEE Computer Society
3 Park Ave., 17th Floor
New York, NY 10016
website: www.ieee.org

The IEEE Computer Society is the world's largest professional organization for advancing technology and engineering globally. It provides many publications, conferences, technology standards, and professional and educational activities that those interested in software development will find useful.

National Association of Programmers
PO Box 529
Prairieville, LA 70769
website: www.napusa.org

The association is for programmers, developers, consultants, and other professionals and students in the computer industry. It provides information and resources for members, including articles, certification, events, and more.

Computer Systems Analyst

While a systems administrator focuses on updating and maintaining the networks associated with a computer system, a systems analyst configures specific software and hardware to solve problems and improve computer systems' performance. Systems analysts study an organization's current computer systems and procedures. They often work closely with business leaders to understand an organization's goals. Merging information technology (IT) and business needs, they design software and hardware systems to achieve these goals.

To do their job, computer systems analysts need to understand how an organization's business works—whether it is a technology company in California or a manufacturing company in Ohio. For example, a manufacturing company needs to track materials through each step of the manufacturing process, from raw materials to finished goods. A health

At a Glance
Computer Systems Analyst

Minimum Educational Requirements

Bachelor's degree

Personal Qualities

Strong analytical, technical, and communications skills

Certification and Licensing

Not required, but can strengthen résumé

Working Conditions

Office environment

Salary Range

Median pay of $85,800 in 2015

Number of Jobs

About 567,800 as of 2014

Future Job Outlook

Projected growth of 21 percent through 2024

care company has different needs, most of which involve tracking patient records. Knowing more about the business allows computer systems analysts to research which computer hardware, software, and networks are most appropriate for improving the organization's computer systems.

When designing a computer system, analysts often use data modeling. Data modeling allows analysts to visualize how a system's processes and data flow. For example, for an inventory costing system, analysts will use data about raw materials and labor hours used during manufacturing. For an investment bank's system, they may use data about customers' financial transactions. After the system's programs have been written, systems analysts test and analyze information from the system to evaluate whether its design works and is efficient. Analysts calculate the memory and speed requirements for the system. They create flowcharts and other diagrams for computer programmers and engineers to use when building the system. Many analysts also do some programming. After the system is built, they work with programmers and other information technology personnel to solve any problems.

Many computer systems analysts are generalists and work with all types of systems and businesses. Some specialize in certain types of systems or businesses. For example, analysts at an investment bank might work exclusively with financial systems that track customer accounts, investments, financial transactions, and fees. Systems designers or architects specialize in helping organizations select the right hardware and software systems for their needs. For example, a hotel might need an online reservation system. Software quality assurance analysts perform extensive testing on websites and software to make sure they meet the company's requirements. They document any issues and make sure errors are corrected. Programmer analysts combine the jobs of software developer and system analyst. They design system software programs and create applications for an organization. They are also responsible for testing software and debugging problems. This type of analyst generally does more coding than other types of systems analysts.

Bettina Bair is a computer systems analyst. She says that much of her day is spent talking with people in her organization who use computer systems. "I help them tell the programmers what kinds of new programs to build, and after the program is done, I help them learn to use it and get any problems fixed," she says in a Mycooljob .org interview. She says she serves as a liaison between the system's users and the IT department. "Twenty or thirty years ago, users had to learn to talk like a techy in order to get any sort of computer development done. Now that computer systems have gotten more and more complex, it really helps to have a Systems Analyst working with users and programmer as a sort of go-between."

How Do You Become a Computer Systems Analyst?

Education

Most computer systems analysts have at least a bachelor's degree from a four-year college or university in computer systems analysis, computer science, computer information systems, management information systems, business intelligence, or a related field. Because systems analysts must also understand an organization's business side, it is also helpful to take a broad array of marketing, management, finance, and accounting courses. Some computer systems analysts also have a masters' degree in business administration or a related field, with a concentration in information systems. Some analysts who work in technically complex positions also have a master's degree in computer science. After graduating, most computer systems analysts continue to take courses to keep their technical and programming skills up-to-date with the latest technologies.

While most computer systems analysts have a computer-related degree, it is not always required. Some analysts have a bachelor's degree in another field but have acquired technical programming skills and expertise from online classes or other experiences.

Certification and Licensing

Although there are no required certifications or licenses to become a computer systems analyst, some voluntary training and certifications can improve your chances of landing a job or getting promoted. System manufacturers, educational organizations, and professional organizations offer a variety of different certifications. For example, the Institute for Certification of Computing Professionals offers an Information System Analyst certificate. Certificate programs typically feature courses that include the basic principles and strategies used by systems analysts. Certifications for specific systems often include in-depth training on the system's layout, design, and configuration.

Rich Hein, the senior managing editor of *CIO* magazine, urges all IT professionals to consider earning voluntary certificates in order to demonstrate their skill and commitment to the field. "Certifications play an important part of any IT professional's career," he said in a 2012 article on CIO.com. "Certifications are like most things in life: The more you put into them, the more you will get out. . . . Certifications also indicate to employers that you take your job seriously and that you are knowledgeable on the respective technology."

Volunteer Work and Internships

Students interested in this field can learn about it by volunteering for local companies, nonprofit organizations, and government entities. In this way students can gain related work experience and demonstrate leadership and managerial skills that will help them stand out.

Many students also work in an internship to gain experience and skills. David Gutierrez, a student at the University of Washington, worked as an intern for Starbucks. He helped develop user interfaces for a new internal software program. "I had to use my skills from informatics and my focus on HCI (human-computer interaction), and think about how a user would go about using this software," he says in an article on the University of Washington website. "I was learning a ton of different things—the role of a systems analyst, how to lead meetings effectively, how to present to higher ups in the company, organizational skills, and leadership skills." At the end of his internship, Gutierrez gave a presentation to management summarizing his work. He was also offered a full-time position as a systems analyst at Starbucks after graduation.

Skills and Personality

Computer systems analysts need a good mix of technical, analytical, and business skills to be successful. They must be able to understand and interpret complex information from different sources and determine the most effective and efficient way to design a system. Creativity is also important, as analysts must be able to think of unique solutions to computer problems and needs.

Systems analysts also need to be effective and efficient communicators. They rely on their expert communication skills when they discuss issues with management and the IT department. They must be able to explain technical and business issues in a way that both will understand. All such analysts require the ability to speak well, listen to others, and write clearly and effectively. These skills can help a candidate stand out. "Coming out of [school], we all have similar skills," says Gutierrez. "It's how you apply those skills that really makes you marketable. Communication and your personality goes a long way."

Systems analysts must also understand the business field in which they work. For example, an analyst for a hospital should know about the health care industry and be familiar with insurance billing practices and patient record data. An analyst for a bank should have background knowledge of finance, including how interest is calculated, loan repayment plans, and investment portfolios.

On the Job

Employers and Working Conditions

According to the Bureau of Labor Statistics (BLS), there were about 567,800 computer systems analysts in 2014. Some systems analysts work directly for companies, while others work as consultants. Consultants usually work for an IT firm that contracts with client companies to provide IT services. According to the BLS, the industries that employed the most computer systems analysts in 2014 were computer systems design and related services (27 percent), finance and insurance (13 percent), information (8 percent), and state and local government (7 percent).

Most projects require computer systems analysts to collaborate and work with others on a team. Most analysts work in an office, although some telecommute from home. Those who work as consultants travel to their clients' offices. Most systems analysts work full time. Sometimes systems analysts are required to work in the evening or on weekends in order to meet project deadlines. In 2014 about 20 percent reported working more than forty hours per week.

Earnings

According to the BLS, as of May 2015 the median annual pay for a computer systems analyst was $85,800. Depending on the industry and organization, earnings can vary. In 2014 wages ranged from less than $51,910 to more than $135,450 for the highest-paid analysts.

In addition, computer systems analysts typically receive other benefits, which can amount to thousands of dollars. Benefits vary from employer to employer and can include paid vacation and sick leave, bonuses, medical and dental insurance, education benefits and tuition reimbursement, retirement benefits, and life insurance.

Opportunities for Advancement

With experience, some computer systems analysts can advance to positions that have additional responsibilities and leadership roles. They may become a project manager and lead a team of system analysts. Others advance to higher-level positions, such as IT director or chief technology officer, which is an executive-level position that focuses on technological issues.

Experienced analysts who demonstrate a record of excellent performance and effective leadership are more likely to be promoted. Earning professional certifications or a master's degree in business administration with a focus on information systems or a related field can also help.

What Is the Future Outlook for Computer Systems Analysts?

The job outlook for computer systems analysts is very good. According to the BLS's *Occupational Outlook Handbook*, employment of computer systems analysts is projected to grow 21 percent from 2014 to 2024. This growth rate is much faster than the average rate for all occupations.

One of the main drivers of growth for this career is the fact that organizations around the world increasingly rely on IT. Computer systems analysts will be needed to design and install new systems. Smaller organizations may find it cheaper to hire outside analysts to help with their systems, which will increase opportunities for consultants.

The health care field is expected to be a main driver of job growth in this area. As health care organizations move toward using electronic health records, e-prescriptions, and other technologies, computer systems analysts will be needed to design, install, and maintain the necessary systems.

Because of the high salary, competition for computer systems analyst positions is typically strong. Candidates with strong technical skills and a background in business will have the best prospects, as will those who have familiarity with a job's specific field or industry.

Find Out More

Association for Computing Machinery
2 Penn Plaza, Suite 701
New York, NY 10121
website: www.acm.org

This organization provides resources such as publications, conferences, and career resources for system analysts and other IT professionals. It has members worldwide and encourages networking and sharing of information to strengthen the IT profession and industry.

CompTIA
3500 Lacey Rd., Suite 100
Downers Grove, IL 60515
website: www.comptia.org

CompTIA provides many IT certifications and education resources for professionals in IT, including systems analysts. The organization also advocates for the IT industry at the local, state, and federal government levels.

Computing Research Association
1828 L St. NW, Suite 800
Washington, DC 20036
website: http://cra.org

This organization works to bring industry, government, and academic professionals together to improve research and education in computing. Its website has news articles, research reports, best practice memos, and job opportunities of interest to systems analysts and other IT professionals.

IEEE Computer Society
3 Park Ave., 17th Floor
New York, NY 10016
website: www.ieee.org

The IEEE Computer Society is the world's largest professional organization for advancing technology and engineering globally. It provides many publications, conferences, technology standards, and professional and educational activities that are of interest to systems analysts.

Network Systems Administrator

At a Glance
Network Systems Administrator

Minimum Educational Requirements
Bachelor's degree

Personal Qualities
Strong technical, analytical, and communication skills, attention to detail

Certification and Licensing
Preferred

Working Conditions
Office environment

Salary Range
Median pay of $77,810 in 2015

Number of Jobs
About 382,600 as of 2014

Future Job Outlook
Projected growth of 8 percent through 2024

While computer systems analysts configure and design software and hardware systems, network systems administrators are responsible for keeping an organization's computer networks up-to-date and running smoothly. Any organization that uses multiple systems or software platforms needs people to coordinate the different systems so they work together. Network systems administrators do this important job. They are responsible for planning, installing, maintaining, and upgrading systems such as local area networks, wide area networks, network segments, intranets, and data communication systems. In addition, network systems administrators make sure an organization's networks are free of viruses and other malware.

When a problem arises in any of the hardware or software that runs the organization's networks, the systems administrator leaps into action to correct the problem swiftly. In addition, systems administrators are responsible for updating all equipment and software, making sure that e-mail and data storage networks are operating properly, and connecting employee workstations to the organization's computer network. They set up and maintain the organizations' servers and train new users to use various hardware and software. Some systems administrators manage the organization's telecommunications networks. This lets employees connect to the central network even when they work from home or are traveling. In some organizations, network systems administrators help make decisions about which hardware and software the company should buy. They may also provide technical support to users.

Russ Gillespie is a network systems administrator at Madgex, a software company based in the United Kingdom. He spends most of his time solving problems that the system's users encounter, such as a web browser not working or a network being slow to respond to user requests. When he arrives at work, Gillespie checks several monitoring systems to make sure no pressing issues have arisen with the company's various systems. If anything has surfaced, he works immediately to resolve the problem. He says that being able to quickly switch from one piece of work to another is a valuable skill for his position. "Over the years I've had to become an absolute master task switcher," he explains in a 2013 interview on the Madgex website. "If I'm working through a problem and the phone rings, I've got to answer it. It might be a quick job, and if it is I might as well do it straight away. I have a three minute rule: If something will take me less than three minutes, I do it immediately. If not, it gets queued up [put in line]."

How Do You Become a Network Systems Administrator?

Education

Most network systems administrators have at least a bachelor's degree in computer or information science. Some degree programs specifically focus on computer network and system administration.

A network systems administrator keeps a company's computer networks up-to-date and running smoothly. This person is essential for companies that use multiple systems or software platforms that have to work together.

Degrees in computer engineering or electrical engineering—in which one gets experience working with computer hardware and equipment—are also acceptable. Students in these programs will typically take courses in computer programming, networking, and systems design. Some companies prefer network systems administrators to have a master's degree.

Those who work in this field need to keep up with the latest technologies and industry developments. To do so, they take continuing education courses throughout their careers and attend industry conferences. "It's imperative to stay current with technology trends and changes by reading blogs, technology magazines and attending conferences," says Simran Sandhu, manager of network infrastructure at the computer software company Adobe Systems. As he says in an article posted on the *U.S. News & World Report* website, "It's also important to study and learn the basics of network technology and acquire an acute understanding of how information flows."

Certification and Licensing

Many employers prefer network systems administrators to have certifications in the products they use. Many vendors offer such programs. For example, Microsoft and Cisco offer certifications for their various network devices, such as servers, routers, and operating systems. Obtaining these certifications demonstrates an employee's commitment to acquiring new skills and confirms his or her existing ones.

Although many certifications are available, the process for obtaining each one is similar. Students must have a certain level of experience and pass an exam. Sajith Balan, a network engineer for Microsoft Network Design and Deployment, has completed several certificate programs. "That really helped me to get a good grip on the role that I have today," he says in an article posted on the *U.S. News & World Report* website. "There are a lot of new technologies that are coming into the market every day, so you have to be conscious of what is happening, and you need to keep learning. Keep your certifications updated."

Volunteer Work and Internships

Doing an internship can help students learn more about this career. Internships allow students to observe and participate in the day-to-day work, as well as make contacts for future job opportunities. Many schools have a list of companies that hire interns or a program that has an internship component.

Ross Sabolcik is a senior software engineer at National Instruments, which makes computer equipment and software. He recommends that all computer science students try to find an internship while in school. Doing so will give them an idea of what it is really like to work in computer science, as he learned during his own internship. "The thing that was valuable about it was seeing what people really do on a day-to-day basis," he says in an interview posted on the Career Cornerstone Center website. He suggests that students ask a lot of questions when they intern. "'What classes did you find really valuable?' or 'What skills do you think I need?' or 'What do you recommend?' The main thing is just getting feedback from people who are actually doing the work."

Skills and Personality

Successful network systems administrators have strong technical and analytical skills. These help them evaluate network and system performance and figure out how changes in hardware, software, and other variables will affect performance.

Sidney Rankin works as a systems engineer at TASC Inc. in Virginia. She says that problem solving and math are particularly relevant to her job. "The basic skills I use day to day are the problem-solving skills that you learn in math and the analytical thinking," she says in an interview posted on the Career Cornerstone Center website. "And also when [you're] programming . . . you're going to come across problem[s] that you need to do calculations [to solve]. So that's where math definitely comes into play." As a project manager, Rankin also tracks the budget for each project, which also involves math.

Network systems administrators must also be able to juggle several tasks at once. This helps them oversee and manage many types of computer hardware and software and make sure everything works together. As different problems arise, network systems administrators must be able to evaluate and prioritize issues and tasks.

Finally, systems administrators must be effective and efficient communicators. They rely on their expert communication skills when they discuss network issues and solutions with management and the information technology (IT) department. They must be able to explain technical issues in a way that non-IT personnel will understand. All such analysts require the ability to speak well, listen to others, and write clearly and effectively. These skills can help a candidate stand out from other applicants.

On the Job

Employers and Working Conditions

According to the Bureau of Labor Statistics (BLS), there were approximately 382,600 network systems administrators working in 2014. Systems administrators work in many industries, including educational services, finance and insurance, and manufacturing. They are typically found in an office environment or wherever the organization's physical computer networks and systems are located. Some administrators work for computer system design firms that contract with other companies to fill their IT needs.

Most systems administrators work full time, or forty hours per week. Because computer networks are critical to an organization's success and functioning, systems administrators often work overtime to resolve any problems and make sure that all networks are working smoothly. Because they are always on call, systems administrators might work evenings and weekends, especially during a technical emergency. According to the BLS, about 25 percent of systems administrators worked more than forty hours per week in 2014.

Earnings

According to the BLS, as of May 2015 the median annual pay for network systems administrators was $77,810. The lowest-paid 10 percent earned less than $47,460, while the highest-paid 10 percent earned more than $124,090. Network systems administrators typically receive other benefits too, which can amount to thousands of dollars. Benefits vary from employer to employer and often include paid vacation and sick leave, bonuses, medical and dental insurance, education and tuition reimbursement benefits, retirement benefits, and life insurance.

Opportunities for Advancement

Network systems administrators can advance to positions that have more responsibility. They may supervise others in the IT department, such as computer and information systems managers. Others become computer network architects, who design and build an organization's networks.

Network systems administrators are likely to be promoted if they demonstrate a thorough knowledge of their organization, its systems, and technical requirements. Earning voluntary professional certifications or a master's degree in computer science or a related field can also improve your opportunities to advance.

What Is the Future Outlook for Network Systems Administrators?

According to the BLS's *Occupational Outlook Handbook*, network systems administrator jobs are projected to increase 8 percent from 2014 to 2024. This growth rate is about the same as the average rate for all occupations.

Employment growth in this career is being driven by the fact that organizations are constantly investing in faster technology and mobile networks. For example, as the health care industry increases its use of IT to create electronic records and facilitate billing and other processes, more systems administrators will be needed to manage systems at hospitals and other such organizations. In addition, as more small and medium-sized organizations outsource their IT departments, the demand for network systems administrators who work for IT consulting companies is also expected to increase.

Overall, job prospects for network systems administrators are expected to be good. Candidates who have a bachelor's degree, voluntary certifications, and related work experience will have the best prospects for landing a job in this field.

Find Out More

Association for Computing Machinery
2 Penn Plaza, Suite 701
New York, NY 10121
website: www.acm.org

This organization provides publications, conferences, career resources, and more for network systems administrators and other IT professionals. It has members worldwide and encourages networking and sharing of information to strengthen the profession and industry.

CompTIA
3500 Lacey Rd., Suite 100
Downers Grove, IL 60515
website: www.comptia.org

CompTIA provides many IT certifications and education resources for professionals in information technology, including network systems administrators. The organization also advocates for the IT industry at the local, state, and federal government levels.

IEEE Computer Society
3 Park Ave., 17th Floor
New York, NY 10016
website: www.ieee.org

The IEEE Computer Society is the world's largest professional organization for advancing technology and engineering globally. It provides many publications, conferences, technology standards, and professional and educational activities that are helpful for network systems administrators.

Network Professional Association (NPA)
3517 Camino Del Rio S., Suite 215
San Diego, CA 92108
website: www.npa.org

The NPA is an organization for network computing professionals, including systems administrators. It provides information and education for network professionals through conferences, workshops, seminars, publications, and other networking events.

Database Administrator

What Does a Database Administrator Do?

Data has become many companies' most valuable asset. Organizations rely on customer data, financial data, product data, and other types of data as they track customer purchases, analyze financial transactions, and seek the most efficient production methods. The job of storing and protecting an organization's data falls to its database administrators (DBAs). DBAs use specialized software to store and organize large amounts of information so it can be easily accessed and interpreted by authorized users. DBAs put security measures in place to make sure that sensitive data cannot be accessed by people who are not supposed to see it.

One of a DBA's main responsibilities is to set up a database that meets a company's needs and make sure it operates efficiently. DBAs work with company management to understand what type of data a company needs to collect, who will use it, and for what. Using this information, DBAs can determine

At a Glance

Database Administrator

Minimum Educational Requirements
Bachelor's degree

Personal Qualities
Strong analytical, logical-thinking, and problem-solving skills; attention to detail

Certification and Licensing
Highly recommended

Working Conditions
Office environment

Salary Range
Median pay of $81,710 in 2015

Number of Jobs
About 120,000 as of 2014

Future Job Outlook
Projected growth of 11 percent through 2024

the best way to set up the database, sometimes collaborating with computer and information systems managers to do so.

Once a database is established, a DBA monitors its performance and modifies it as needed. Because many databases hold sensitive information (such as financial or personal data), securing it is a key priority. DBAs also back up the systems so no data will be lost if there is a power outage or other disaster. They also test the integrity of the database, making sure the data it contains comes from a reliable source.

While many DBAs work on all aspects of data storage and security, some DBAs specialize in certain areas. System DBAs specialize in a database's physical and technical parts. They install upgrades and patches to fix bugs, or errors. These specialists often have experience in system architecture, which is a conceptual model or blueprint of a system, including its physical components, relationships, functions, and rules. Application DBAs work with databases that have been set up for a specific software program, such as customer service software. They are well versed in how to use the programs that work with the database.

Bruce Nation is a DBA for CoverMyMeds, a health care technology company. In an interview on the company's website, he says, "My job is to make certain all the data behind our applications is stored safely and is quickly accessible. Our team spends a lot of time performance tuning, working with developers to structure the data properly and planning for worst case scenarios." Nation is trained to think of all kinds of scenarios. "We need to be prepared for situations like losing our databases because of disk corruption," he says. "Or if a meteor hits our datacenter." He says the best part of his job is the ability to help others and come up with creative solutions. "I love problem-solving," he continues. "Figuring out how to get patients their medications faster is the big one, but underneath that there are many layers of smaller problems that we work on every day."

How Do You Become a DBA?

Education

Most DBAs have at least a bachelor's degree from a four-year college or university. They typically major in management information

Storing and protecting a company's data is the job of a database administrator. This tech professional sets up a company's database, makes sure it runs smoothly, and institutes security measures to protect sensitive data.

systems or a computer-related field. Organizations with large databases may require administrators to have a master's degree in computer science, information systems, or information technology. When pursuing these degrees, students will need to take classes in database languages, such as Structured Query Language.

Many DBAs also have several years of related work experience in database development or data analysis. Database developers are software developers who create databases, while data analysts interpret the information stored in a database. After gaining experience in these positions, a candidate can move into database administration.

Certification and Licensing

Certification is highly recommended for DBAs. Some companies require DBAs to be certified in certain products that the organization uses. Obtaining certifications can improve a person's chances of landing a job or getting promoted. April Miller Cripliver, an associate professor at Ivy Tech Community College in Indiana, holds more than twenty-five computer certifications in networking, security, hardware, and operating systems. "The IT [information technology] landscape changes almost constantly," she says in a 2015 article in *Certification Magazine*. "Keeping up with technology is important, and certifications can certainly demonstrate that you're staying current."

Many companies that sell or license database programs—such as Microsoft and Oracle—offer database certifications. To earn one, candidates must have a certain level of experience and pass a series of tests. Many students prepare for certification exams by studying, doing online and traditional class work, and getting hands-on lab experience.

Volunteer Work and Internships

Students interested in this career can learn more about the field by doing an internship. Interning helps students get related work experience and demonstrate leadership and technical skills. While studying computer science engineering at the University of Michigan, Mike McGookey worked as an intern in the school's information and technology services department. In an interview on the University of Michigan website, McGookey describes his experience:

> I am working on a few different projects for my department. They include building a Google Site to house the team's resources, editing and writing . . . scripts for database maintenance, and researching a package management system for synchronizing database settings across servers. I am also working on a project with other interns creating a tool that allows for recently graduated students to copy files out of [the database] and onto their local computer.

Skills and Personality

Successful DBAs have solid analytical, logical-thinking, and problem-solving skills. They need to make sense of all of the data that goes into a database and organize it in a clear and meaningful way so it can be easily retrieved when needed. They must be able to monitor and analyze a database's performance and evaluate complex systems. Working with databases can be complex, and small errors can cause big problems. To prevent costly mistakes, administrators must be extremely detail oriented.

Because DBAs often work on several projects at once, they need to be able to juggle several tasks and deadlines at the same time. "You must be very good at multitasking, you need to have a strong attention to detail and good time-management skills," says Loretta Mahon Smith, former vice president of communications for DAMA International, a nonprofit association for technical and business professionals, in an article for *U.S. News & World Report*.

On the Job

Employers and Working Conditions

DBAs work in many industries, including educational services, health care, and retail. While some work directly for large organizations, many work for data hosting and data processing firms that contract out services to other companies. Others work for companies that use large databases, such as insurance companies and banks. These financial firms track enormous amounts of personal and financial data for their customers. Other DBAs work for retail companies that need to track shopping and credit card data or health care organizations that track patients' medical and insurance data.

Most DBAs work full time, and about 20 percent worked more than forty hours per week in 2014, according to the Bureau of Labor Statistics (BLS). DBAs are often on call, which means they can be called in to solve a problem at any time, day or night. "Be prepared to work long hours—sometimes in the middle of the night or on holiday weekends," says Craig Mullins, a data management strategist for BMC Software, in an article posted on the Monster website. "Although many database maintenance tasks are becoming more flexible, DBAs still need to be available to perform administrative operations during off-hours to minimize downtime during critical hours. This means working at less-than-desirable times."

Earnings

According to the BLS, as of May 2015 the median annual pay for DBAs was $81,710. In 2014 wages ranged from less than $45,460 to more than $127,080 for the highest-paid administrators. DBAs who work for an organization or consulting firm typically receive other benefits, which can amount to thousands of dollars. Benefits vary from employer to employer. These can include paid vacation and sick leave, bonuses, medical and dental insurance, education benefits and tuition reimbursement, retirement benefits, and life insurance.

Opportunities for Advancement

Experienced DBAs generally have the opportunity to take on more complex projects. Senior-level administrators may become IT managers and supervise teams working on a large project. IT project managers plan and direct an organization's technology activities. They help an organization set goals and put into place the computer systems and technologies needed to meet those goals.

Experienced DBAs who demonstrate a record of excellent performance are more likely to be promoted. Earning professional certifications or a master's degree in computer science or a related field can also improve a person's opportunities to advance.

What Is the Future Outlook for DBAs?

The job outlook for DBAs is very good. According to the BLS's *Occupational Outlook Handbook*, DBA jobs are projected to grow 11 percent from 2014 to 2024. This growth rate is faster than the average rate for all other occupations.

As companies across all industries increasingly rely on all types of data, DBAs will be needed to organize, access, and protect this data. In addition, an increase in cloud computing and database administration by third-party service providers is projected to increase demand for administrators who work in data processing, hosting, and related services industries. As more small and medium-size organizations outsource their IT departments to consulting companies, these consulting firms are expected to hire more and more DBAs. Also, as health care organizations use more electronic records, they will need more databases—and administrators to manage them—to track patient data.

DBAs are highly sought-after employees, and some organizations have difficulty finding enough qualified candidates to fill open positions. Those who have extensive work experience and are up-to-date on the latest technologies will have the best prospects for landing a job in this field.

Find Out More

Association for Computing Machinery
2 Penn Plaza, Suite 701
New York, NY 10121
website: www.acm.org

This organization provides resources such as publications, conferences, and career resources that are useful for many IT professionals, including DBAs. It has members worldwide and encourages networking and sharing of information to strengthen the profession and industry.

Association of Information Technology Professionals (AITP)
1120 Route 73, Suite 200
Mount Laurel, NJ 08054
website: www.aitp.org

The AITP works to advance the information technology profession through professional development, education, and national policies. It features webinars, conferences, awards for professionals and students, a career center with a jobs board, and networking options for all IT professionals, including DBAs. It has chapters for professionals and students across the United States.

DAMA International
364 E. Main St., Suite 157
Middletown, DE 19709
website: www.dama.org

DAMA International is a global association of professionals involved with information and data management. The DAMA website offers links to educational webinars, information about career paths, and networking opportunities for data professionals.

Institute for Certification of Computing Professionals (ICCP)
2400 E. Devon Ave., Suite 281
Des Plaines, IL 60018
website: www.iccp.org

The ICCP offers numerous certifications for computer and data professionals. It also has several online study, self-study, and other educational programs to prepare candidates for certification exams.

Web Developer

It is hard to think of a contemporary company or organization that does *not* have a website. Customers visit a company's website to learn more about products, find store locations, and buy products online. In turn, companies and organizations use their websites to advertise their services, publicize their activities, and raise awareness about certain causes, missions, or endeavors. Designing a website that meets these needs is the job of web developers.

Website developers create the layout, color scheme, and general design of websites. They create specialized, eye-catching websites for many industries. They are also responsible for a site's technical aspects, including its performance (speed) and capacity (traffic). They may work for a company or organization directly or be hired independently. Because every organization is different, web developers work with each client to create an individual design. They consider a client's products and services when designing the site. After the site is

At a Glance

Web Developer

Minimum Educational Requirements
Associate's degree

Personal Qualities
Creative, attention to detail, strong interpersonal skills

Certification and Licensing
Not required, but can strengthen résumé

Working Conditions
Office environment

Salary Range
Median pay of $64,970 in 2015

Number of Jobs
About 148,500 in 2014

Future Job Outlook
Projected growth of 27 percent through 2024

42

built, they regularly adjust and add updates to the site. In some cases web developers also create content for the site.

In a typical day, web developers might meet with clients or management to discuss a site's needs and design. Once they determine what the client wants, they get to work designing the site. They might write code using programming languages such as HTML or XML. They may write and test applications, such as shopping carts, product support forums, or log-in pages. They may meet with other team members to determine a site's layout, what information it will impart, and what graphics will appear. Developers may also integrate graphics, audio, and video into a website. Once they have finished designing and building a test site, a developer will meet with the client to review and approve what has been built. Once the site is approved, it goes live on the Internet. After the site is up and running, a web developer might monitor user traffic on the site and suggest improvements to the site's design.

Because every website is different, web developers customize each site for their clients' needs. For example, a website for a bank needs applications that allow customers to use online banking features. In contrast, a website for a health care organization might focus on hospital and research news and allow users to search for doctors and book appointments. Together the web developer and client decide which applications a site needs. "We don't use any templates," says Garry Kanfer, president of Big Drop Inc., a New York City web design and development company. In an article posted on the *U.S. News & World Report* website, he explains, "We start from a blank canvas, and the client has to approve everything page by page."

Some web developers build an entire website from start to finish. Others specialize in a particular area of web development. Back-end web developers work on the site's technical construction. They create its framework and make sure it works as designed. They also add procedures for others to add pages and content in the future. Front-end developers focus on a site's appearance. They design the layout and integrate graphics and other content. Once a website is live, webmasters maintain and update the site. They monitor it to make sure everything is working properly and respond to user comments and questions.

How Do You Become a Web Developer?

Education

There is no standard educational path for a career as a web developer. People who want to work in this field should have strong computer skills and a knowledge of graphic design. Taking courses in programming languages such as HTML and CSS can hone the necessary skills for this career. In addition, knowing JavaScript or Structured Query Language and computer programs such as Outlook, Adobe Photoshop, Flash FXP, and Microsoft Project is very beneficial. Courses in graphic design are also helpful, especially if the developer will be working primarily on a site's appearance. Because technology changes rapidly, web developers are expected to keep up-to-date on the latest tools and programming languages.

Some candidates enroll in an associate's degree program in web design or development. Students in these programs learn computer basics along with more challenging content such as web animation and multimedia design. For very technical positions—such as a back-end web developer—some companies may prefer candidates who have a bachelor's degree in computer science, programming, or a related field. For positions that focus on a website's appearance, companies may prefer a candidate who has both a computer degree and course work in graphic design. When applying for jobs, web developers are expected to provide a portfolio of web work they have completed.

Certification and Licensing

Although web developers do not need any special licenses, undergoing training or getting certifications can improve your chances of landing a job or getting promoted. Certification courses, training seminars, and courses organized by professional societies and universities can show you are committed to improving your knowledge and skills. Common web development certifications include Certified Web Developer, Certified Internet Webmaster, Advanced Web Developer, and Mobile Application Development.

Volunteer Work and Internships

Many web developers do an internship, either paid or unpaid, to build up their portfolio of work. To get started, some people volunteer to design a website for a local charity. Web designer Haris Bacic explains in a 2014 article posted on the *Forbes* website:

> While most charities don't have big budgets to work with, everyone loves getting stuff for free. Call or meet with a few of your local charities and talk to them. They might need their website redesigned, or a new logo, or even some brochures. Whatever they might need, you could offer it to them. And not only will it help build your portfolio, they might actually recommend you to real companies and bring you business.

With a few examples of their work, candidates can apply for internships, some of which pay. "I started off my internship getting paid about $15 an hour and that comes in handy if you're still going to school and need to pay tuition and expenses," says Bacic. He recommends that students not be too selective when choosing an internship, because internships are really just about building a portfolio. "It's OK to look for internships that aren't exact fits with your ideal goals or visions," he says. "Internships are just meant to give you real-world experience and help you polish your skills. You're not going to be there forever."

Skills and Personality

Successful web developers are creative, pay close attention to details, and have strong interpersonal skills. They must come up with creative designs for their clients' sites and make sure the sites are innovative and feature the most up-to-date apps and graphics. Building these sites can be tedious. Therefore, developers need patience and the ability to concentrate and sit in front of a computer for long periods. In addition, they must be extremely detail oriented. A tiny mistake in one section of the site's code can cause problems throughout the entire site.

Web developers also spend a lot of their time working with other team members, clients, and the site's users. This makes it important to have strong interpersonal skills and to work well with people of all backgrounds.

Employers and Working Conditions

Web developers are needed to develop websites for companies and organizations across many industries. While some work directly for large organizations, many work for computer systems design firms that contract with companies to do special projects like web development. Others are self-employed and work on a project-by-project basis. According to the Bureau of Labor Statistics (BLS), there were approximately 148,500 web developers working in 2014. The industries that employed the most web developers were computer systems design and other related services (20 percent); educational services (7 percent); religious, grant-making, civic, professional, and similar organizations (5 percent); and other information services (5 percent). Most of the time, web developers work in an office, and most work full time. In addition, the job can involve travel to meet with clients.

Earnings

According to the BLS, as of May 2015 the median annual pay for web developers was $64,970. Earnings vary across organizations. In 2014 wages ranged from less than $34,770 to more than $116,620 for the highest-paid developers.

In addition, web developers who work for an organization or consulting firm typically receive other benefits, which can amount to thousands of dollars. Benefits vary from employer to employer. These benefits can include paid vacation and sick leave, bonuses, medical and dental insurance, education benefits and tuition reimbursement, retirement benefits, and life insurance.

Opportunities for Advancement

Experienced web developers usually get to take on more responsibility and work on complex projects, such as building a new web application system that allows clients to make edits to their sites. Web developers with a bachelor's degree and experience may supervise teams of developers on a large project. Some developers may advance to higher-level positions, such as project managers. Others might leave an organization and start their own consulting company.

Experienced web developers with a track record of excellent work are more likely to be considered for a promotion. In addition, those who have earned professional certifications or a bachelor's degree are also more likely to have more opportunities to advance.

What Is the Future Outlook for Web Developers?

The job outlook for web developers is very good. According to the BLS's *Occupational Outlook Handbook*, web developer jobs are projected to grow 27 percent from 2014 to 2024. This growth rate is much faster than the average rate for all occupations.

As the Internet becomes more integrated into daily life and e-commerce expands, the need for websites and web developers is expected to be strong. The increase in mobile device use is one factor driving job growth for this career. Web developers will be needed to create websites that work on mobile devices with many different screen sizes. Web developers who have experience using multiple programming languages and multimedia tools will have the best opportunities.

Because websites can be built anywhere, some web developer jobs may be moved to other countries, where wages are lower. However, the cost of managing developers in multiple countries may offset any wage savings, which could encourage organizations to hire developers closer to home. In addition, local web developers are better able to understand cultural nuances and design websites that communicate most effectively with users. For example, studies have shown that users in China may be more responsive to web designs that feature pictures of groups instead of individuals and male subjects rather than female subjects. Therefore, web designers need to be culturally literate; this may limit the movement of web development jobs overseas.

Find Out More

Association of Web Design Professionals
website: www.awdp.org

A global directory of web design businesses, the group's website also provides information about job listings, tech careers, and industry news.

International Web Association (IWA)
119 E. Union St., Suite #A
Pasadena, CA 91103
website: http://iwanet.org

The IWA is the industry's recognized leader in providing educational and certification standards for web professionals. The association supports more than three hundred thousand individual members in 106 countries.

Web Professionals
PO Box 584
Washington, IL 61571
website: webprofessionals.org

Web Professionals is a nonprofit professional association dedicated to supporting individuals and organizations who create, manage, or market websites. The association's website provides education and training resources as well as certification resources for web development professionals.

Computer Hardware Engineer

What Does a Computer Hardware Engineer Do?

At a Glance

Computer Hardware Engineer

Minimum Educational Requirements
Bachelor's degree

Personal Qualities
Strong communication, critical-thinking, and problem-solving skills; creativity

Certification and Licensing
Not required, but can strengthen résumé

Working Conditions
Office environment

Salary Range
Median pay of $111,730 in 2015

Number of Jobs
About 77,700 as of 2014

Future Job Outlook
Projected growth of 3 percent through 2024

Every computer system is made up of many components, such as processors, circuit boards, memory devices, networks, and routers. Computer hardware engineers are responsible for overseeing the design, manufacture, installation, and testing of computer hardware and equipment. *Hardware* refers to a computer system's physical components, including its motherboard, processor, storage drives, and media drives. People in this job also work with peripheral equipment such as keyboards and printers. These professionals keep up-to-date on the latest developments and releases in computer technology and evaluate how these can help an organization.

In addition to tending to an organization's equipment, computer hardware engineers also help design new equipment. To do this, they often work closely with software developers to design the hardware and software that operate together. In some cases hardware engineers may also do some computer programming; they often work in a hardware description language (HDL). Using HDL, hardware engineers can model and simulate how a design would work. They then test for errors and use the feedback to alter and improve the design.

In a typical day, a computer hardware engineer might work on a design for new computer hardware and create a schematic of the proposed equipment. Once a model of the hardware is complete, the engineer will test it and analyze the results. If needed, he or she will go back and adjust the design so it meets expectations. A hardware engineer might also update current computer equipment so it is compatible with new software releases. In some cases he or she will oversee the hardware manufacturing process.

Some computer hardware engineers work with other types of devices that use processors and connect to the Internet. For example, a number of medical devices and car components have computer systems built into them. Computer hardware engineers are responsible for designing these devices and figuring out how they will operate.

Some computer hardware engineers work in research labs to develop and design new hardware and systems. As they design, they consider several factors, including functional requirements, cost, reliability, and safety. They test these products to make sure they meet certain requirements and make modifications if necessary. Through their work, computer hardware engineers contribute to advances in computer technology. These have included developing portable storage devices to transfer large amounts of data between devices and designing faster video graphics cards to improve the look of video games.

John Harding is a hardware development engineer at Hewlett-Packard. He spends a lot of time developing new hardware designs. In an interview posted on the TryEngineering website, Harding says he loves being able to work on the devices of the future. "I come in and I play with next generation technology, future technology. We're developing technology here that people won't see for another two, three years," he says. "And that's my job. I get to push the envelope of the technology, and I really like what I do—and secondarily, I'm generously rewarded for it."

Education

Most computer hardware engineers have at least a bachelor's degree in computer engineering from a four-year college or university. Some earn a degree in electrical engineering or computer science. Some employers may prefer to hire applicants who have graduated from an accredited program such as ABET, a nonprofit organization that provides accreditation for college programs in several science and technology areas, including engineering and engineering technology.

In school, students interested in this field should take courses in engineering, math, and science. Yang Ren is a 2017 senior computer engineering major at the University of California–Santa Barbara. At first he did not know much about computer engineering beyond the few computer science classes he took in high school. But Ren knew he enjoyed programming, so he decided to try computer engineering. "I chose Computer Engineering as my major because I wanted to explore the computer hardware and circuit design side of computers that I didn't know anything about," he says in an interview posted on the university's website.

Computer hardware engineering programs will often include classes in computer science, electrical engineering, and mathematics. Students will study software, hardware, networks, and security. Because they often work with computer software systems, students should also take courses in computer science and computer programming.

Some employers may require job candidates to have a master's degree in computer programming. Some hardware engineers opt to get a master's degree in business administration. Geoffrey Fernald is the senior vice president of engineering at the Acuson Corporation in Mountain View, California, where he manages a team of hardware design engineers. Fernald recommends that engineers who want to advance earn a master's degree. "A bachelor's degree puts you too much in the sea of technical people," he says in an interview on the Career Cornerstone website. "I recommend everybody get a Master's degree in order to strengthen the final stages of their technical development."

Because technology changes quickly, hardware engineers need to stay up-to-date on the latest developments in their field by taking courses, attending conferences, and reading industry publications.

Certification and Licensing

For most computer hardware engineers, licensing is optional. However, some jobs require licensing, and if an engineer wants to work as a consultant, he or she will need to be licensed. To get a professional engineer license, computer hardware engineers must graduate from an ABET-accredited program, have several years of work experience, and pass an exam. In addition, some voluntary training and certifications can improve your chance of landing a job or getting promoted. Some computer hardware engineers may get certifications that demonstrate technical ability in a certain area of computer engineering. Many certifications are offered by hardware vendors such as Hewlett-Packard, IBM, and Microsoft.

Volunteer Work and Internships

Students interested in embarking on this career can do an internship while in school; that is a good way to get practical work experience and learn firsthand about the field. In 2015 Karam Namek, an electrical and computer engineering student at Ryerson University in Toronto, Canada, did an internship for Honda of Canada Manufacturing. "My roles and responsibilities include[d] designing hardware systems, programming PLC's [programmable logic controllers], vision systems, teaching robots and commissioning of equipment to meet design specifications, standards and safety regulations," he says in an interview posted on the Ryerson University website. Namek thinks internships have a lot to offer students. "You get the opportunity to apply the theories you are learning in school in a real world engineering environment," he says. "Another great side of internships is the connections you make, the people you meet and work with are a great asset to have as a young engineer."

Skills and Personality

Computer hardware engineers need a range of skills and qualities. They should have strong analytical, critical-thinking, and problem-solving skills and also be fairly creative. Hardware engineers must think outside the box when they consider how to design new devices. At the same time, they must be able to identify complex hardware problems, assess possible solutions, and figure out how to resolve the issue. They also must evaluate different potential solutions and designs, identifying the pros and cons of each before deciding which approach to take.

Computer hardware engineers also need to be effective and efficient communicators. They frequently work on teams with other people and must be able to talk to technical and nontechnical coworkers. All such engineers require the ability to speak well, listen to others, and write clearly and effectively.

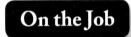

On the Job

Employers and Working Conditions

According to the Bureau of Labor Statistics (BLS), there were about 77,700 computer hardware engineers in 2014. Many work for computer systems design firms (22 percent). Others work for high-tech computer and peripheral equipment manufacturing companies (16 percent), semiconductor and other electronic component manufacturing firms (15 percent), and research and development companies (7 percent).

Most hardware engineers work in a research lab, where they build and test different types of computer hardware models. Most work full time, and approximately 25 percent worked more than forty hours per week in 2014.

Earnings

According to the BLS, as of May 2015 the median annual pay for computer hardware engineers was $111,730. These earnings can vary by organization and a person's experience. In 2014 wages ranged from less than $65,570 to more than $167,100 for the highest-paid managers.

In addition, computer hardware engineers typically receive other benefits, which can amount to thousands of dollars. Benefits vary from employer to employer and can include paid vacation and sick leave, bonuses, medical and dental insurance, education benefits and tuition reimbursement, retirement benefits, and life insurance.

Opportunities for Advancement

Computer hardware engineers who work for larger organizations will have the best opportunities to advance. Some managers move between departments or advance to positions that have additional responsibilities and leadership roles. Others advance to higher-level positions, such as computer and information systems managers, who plan, coordinate, and direct an organization's computer-related activities. Some become chief information officers, senior executives who are responsible for overseeing all of an organization's information technology and computer systems.

Experienced engineers who demonstrate a record of excellent performance are more likely to be promoted. Earning professional certifications or a master's degree in business administration or a related field can also help.

What Is the Future Outlook for Computer Hardware Engineers?

According to the BLS's *Occupational Outlook Handbook*, employment of computer hardware engineers is projected to grow 3 percent from 2014 to 2024. This growth rate is slower than the average rate for all occupations. The limited demand for hardware engineers within the computer industry may be due to the fact that the majority of technological innovation occurs within software rather than hardware. However, as other industries begin to research and develop electronic devices, the need for hardware engineers may increase. For example, as more household appliances, medical devices, and cars get designed with computer chips, hardware engineers will be needed to work on these products.

Although competition for jobs will be strong, hardware engineers with a computer engineering degree from an ABET-accredited program, higher-level degrees, and experience with computer software will have the best job prospects.

Find Out More

Association for Computing Machinery
2 Penn Plaza, Suite 701
New York, NY 10121
website: www.acm.org

This organization provides resources such as publications, conferences, and career advice to information technology (IT) professionals, including computer hardware engineers. It has members worldwide and encourages networking and sharing of information to strengthen the profession and industry.

CompTIA
3500 Lacey Rd., Suite 100
Downers Grove, IL 60515
website: www.comptia.org

CompTIA provides many IT certifications and education resources for professionals in information technology, including computer hardware engineers. The organization also advocates for the IT industry at the local, state, and federal government levels.

Computing Research Association
1828 L St. NW, Suite 800
Washington, DC 20036
website: http://cra.org

This organization works to bring industry, government, and academic professionals together to improve research and education in computing. Its website provides news articles, information about events and conferences, research reports, and best practices for IT professionals, including computer hardware engineers.

IEEE Computer Society
3 Park Ave., 17th Floor
New York, NY 10016
website: www.ieee.org

The IEEE Computer Society is the world's largest professional organization for advancing technology and engineering globally. It provides many publications, conferences, technology standards, and professional and educational activities for all types of IT professionals, including computer hardware engineers.

Information Security Analyst

What Does an Information Security Analyst Do?

At a Glance

Information Security Analyst

Minimum Educational Requirements
Bachelor's degree

Personal Qualities
Strong analytical, critical-thinking, and problem-solving skills; attention to detail

Certification and Licensing
Not required, but can strengthen résumé

Working Conditions
Office environment

Salary Range
Median pay of $90,120 in 2015

Number of Jobs
About 82,900 as of 2014

Future Job Outlook
Projected growth of 18 percent through 2024

Every day more information moves online, including bank statements and other financial information, new product plans, compensation records, and personal information such as passwords, health records, and Social Security numbers. As a result, companies are becoming more vulnerable to data breaches, which occur when hackers attempt to break into company databases and systems to steal information. Such break-ins are a growing problem and cost companies millions of dollars. According to the Ponemon Institute's *2015 Cost of Cyber Crime* report, companies reported an average of 160 successful cyberattacks each week in 2015. The annual cost of these attacks ranged from $1.9 million to $65 million. One of the largest such breaches occurred in 2013, when Adobe Systems executives reported that hackers had broken into the company's internal computer network and stolen the personal information of about 2.9 million customers. The information included customer IDs, encrypted passwords, names, encrypted credit and debit card numbers and expiration dates, and other details from customers' orders. In addition, the hackers stole source code for several of the company's products.

Hackers do several things with the information they steal. They might sell it on the black market, use it to commit identity theft, or use it to directly steal from or otherwise take advantage of their victims. As a result, protecting the information generated by businesses, clients, and consumers has become an enormous task for companies across all industries. Organizations need information security analysts to guard and protect their information systems. These analysts plan security procedures and put security systems into effect. Their goal is to protect

Information security analysts protect an organization's computer systems, networks, and data from cyberattacks, data breaches, and other unauthorized access or usage. They have become valuable members of many workplace teams.

an organization's computer systems, networks, and data from cyberattacks, data breaches, and other unauthorized access or usage.

In a typical day, information security analysts will monitor an organization's networks, looking for signs of a breach. A clear sign might be unusual traffic patterns that may indicate data is leaving the company's network. "It's not just about what comes into your network," according to Sam Erdheim, senior security strategist for AlgoSec, a provider of network security software. "It's about outbound traffic as well," he said in an October 2013 article on the Dark Reading website. Another red flag is changes in a privileged user's account activity. "Changes in the behavior of privileged users can indicate that the user account in question is being used by someone else to establish a beachhead in your network," says Geoff Webb, director of solution strategy for security software company NetIQ. In an October 2013 article on the Dark Reading website, he says, "Watching for changes—such as time of activity, systems accessed, type or volume of information accessed—will provide early indication of a breach."

If analysts suspect a breach has occurred, they will investigate, resolve, document, and report the incident. These analysts also install firewalls and use data encryption programs to protect an organization's data. They simulate attacks on the organization's networks to identify vulnerabilities that need to be fixed. They research the most up-to-date security procedures and products, develop an organization's long-term information security plan, and make recommendations about security to senior management. They also help the company's employees learn to use security products and procedures so they can avoid getting fooled by the many scams that hackers think up to gain access to confidential information.

Although all computer science professionals need to stay up-to-date on the latest industry trends, doing so is particularly critical for information security analysts. As soon as security analysts prevent one type of cyberattack, would-be hackers come up with schemes and tricks to launch another one. As a result, information security analysts need to know the latest types of attacks cybercriminals are launching and what technologies and techniques are being developed to combat them. To do this, they may attend conferences, where they meet with other professionals to discuss new attacks and protection strategies.

Part of this job involves creating a disaster recovery plan for an organization's data and computer systems. If a natural disaster strikes, the organization must be able to recover and restore operations as quickly as possible. This usually involves making regular copies of valuable data and transferring it to a secure, off-site location. Analysts also develop plans to restore computers and networks after a disaster.

Alexis Coupe is a cybersecurity analyst at nbn, an Australian company that designs, builds, and operates Australia's National Broadband Network. He describes his role as a type of cyberpolice. "It's the role of a cyber-analyst to understand the links between security and business threats (such as networks, databases, firewalls, web applications, etc.) and offer proactive and dynamic solutions to identify threats and incidents," he says in an interview posted on the nbn website. Coupe says his favorite part of the job is detecting new threats.

> To be able to do that effectively, we often need to think as an attacker and get creative. When hackers decide to steal confidential documents, they try to make sure that they are not detected by the security team so they can come back in the future. We try and get ahead in the game by simulating those activities and then trying to detect it ourselves. We have the chance to play two different roles in one job (attack and defense) which allow the cyber security analysts to enhance their skills. New security toolkits and techniques are released into market every day. It's a great job where the term "boring" doesn't exist!

How Do You Become an Information Security Analyst?

Education

Most information security analysts have at least a bachelor's degree from a four-year college or university in computer science, computer programming, or a related field. Some schools have specific programs for information security professionals. Some employers require candidates to have a master of business administration in information systems.

Many employers prefer candidates who have related work experience, such as working as a network or systems administrator in an information technology (IT) department. Organizations looking to hire a database security analyst may prefer a candidate who has previously worked as a database administrator, while those looking to hire a systems security analyst may prefer a candidate who has worked as a computer systems analyst.

Certification and Licensing

Although there are no required certifications or licenses for information security analysts, some voluntary training and certifications can improve your chances of landing a job or getting promoted. Some certifications are general, while others specify areas such as penetration testing or systems auditing.

Steve Moulden works as an information security analyst. To prepare for his career, he earned a bachelor's degree in IT with a focus on computer forensics. He also got a master's degree in IT with a focus on Internet security. Moulden believes that ongoing certification is important in his career. "I have several certifications, including CompTIA Security+, and I am awaiting results of my CISSP [Certified Information Systems Security Professional] ," he says in an interview posted on the Utica College website. "The Security+ certification is a great way to get your foot in the door as well. My next certification will be Certified Ethical Hacker."

Volunteer Work and Internships

Many students interested in this field do an internship to gain experience and skills. While a student at the University of Wisconsin–River Falls, Jessica Wilson interned as an IT security analyst during the summer of 2015. "As an Information Systems major, I could not have asked for a better internship," she says in an interview posted on the University of Wisconsin website. "This experience has taught me so much about security operations in today's workplace, from assisting with compliance audit projects to proper implementation of a new company-wide anti-virus software."

Wilson did an internship because it was a valuable way to prepare for a job after college. She liked that it would help her determine whether she would really like a career in the field. "To students seeking a career in any field, IT or other, I can confidently say that the internship experience is second to none in helping students prepare and gain confidence for the real world," she says.

Skills and Personality

Information security analysts need a range of skills and qualities to be successful. They should have strong analytical, critical-thinking, and problem-solving skills. They must be able to identify and analyze security risks and issues, identify and evaluate possible solutions, and figure out the best way to protect an organization's systems and networks. They must also be very detailed oriented. After all, their job is to study systems like a detective, looking for the tiniest sign of a cyberattack or data breach. These breaches may be indicated by changes in network traffic, user account activity, geographical log-in patterns, or numbers of requests for the same file. Such analysts must be extremely ethical, as some parts of the job may involve hacking into systems to highlight areas of weakness that need to be secured.

On the Job

Employers and Working Conditions

Some information security analysts work directly for banks, investment companies, or health care companies. Others work as consultants, usually for an IT company that performs information security work for other companies. According to the Bureau of Labor Statistics (BLS), there were about 82,900 information security analysts in 2014.

Information security analysts frequently collaborate and work with others on a team. Most analysts work in an office, although some telecommute from home. Those who work as consultants travel to their client's offices. Most information security analysts work full time and are usually required to be on call on evenings and weekends in case of an emergency. In 2014 about 25 percent reported working more than forty hours per week.

Earnings

According to the BLS, as of May 2015 the median annual pay for information security analysts was $90,120. Depending on the industry and organization, earnings can vary. In 2014 wages ranged from less than $51,280 to more than $143,770 for the highest-paid analysts. In addition, information security analysts typically receive other employee benefits, which can amount to thousands of dollars.

Opportunities for Advancement

With experience, some information security analysts can advance to positions that have additional responsibilities and leadership roles. They may become a manager and lead a team of analysts. Others advance to higher-level positions such as chief security officer, which is a senior executive position that establishes and maintains an organization's vision, strategy, and programs to make sure IT and data are protected.

What Is the Future Outlook for Information Security Analysts?

The job outlook for information security analysts is very good. According to the BLS's *Occupational Outlook Handbook*, employment of information security analysts is projected to grow 18 percent from 2014 to 2024. This growth rate is much faster than the average rate for all occupations.

As more information is held digitally and the number of cyberattacks and data breaches grow, so too will the need for information security analysts. The federal government is one entity that is expected to significantly increase its demand for information security analysts. These people will be charged with protecting the IT systems that control the country's electricity grid, transportation systems, and other government systems. Health care is another industry with a lot of projected need in this area; as more health care companies use digital medical records, the need to protect them will also grow.

Find Out More

Center for Internet Security (CIS)
31 Tech Valley Dr., Suite 2
East Greenbush, NY 12061
website: www.cisecurity.org

The CIS is a nonprofit organization focused on enhancing the cybersecurity readiness and response of public and private organizations. It provides resources such as reports, seminars, and assessment tools to help organizations achieve security goals.

Information Systems Security Association
11130 Sunrise Valley Dr., Suite 350
Reston, VA 20191
website: www.issa.org

This nonprofit association focuses on providing networking and professional growth options for cybersecurity professionals worldwide. It hosts conferences, organizes local chapters and committees, and distributes information through newsletters and a monthly journal.

International Information Systems Security Certification Consortium (ISC)²
311 Park Place Blvd., Suite 400
Clearwater, FL 33759
website: www.isc2.org

The (ISC)² is a global, not-for-profit leader in educating and certifying information security professionals.

SANS Institute
8120 Woodmont Ave., Suite 310
Bethesda, MD 20814
website: www.sans.org

The SANS Institute is a nonprofit organization that offers computer security training, research, and resources. It develops, maintains, and makes available at no cost a large collection of research documents about various aspects of information security.

Computer Support Specialist

What Does a Computer Support Specialist Do?

As organizations embrace new technologies, employees in all departments must quickly learn how to use computers, software programs, and other types of technology. When they have a problem logging on to their computer or connecting to a company network from home, they call a computer support specialist for help.

Computer support specialists help an organization's employees use their computers and other technology related to their job. No matter what the problem is, computer support specialists must provide quick and friendly assistance. "We need to make sure we know how to diagnose their issues and do it quickly," says Guido Diaz, senior computer support specialist at Florida International University, in an article posted on the *U.S. News & World Report* website. "Customer relations and troubleshooting are very important."

At a Glance

Computer Support Specialist

Minimum Educational Requirements
Associate's degree

Personal Qualities
Strong interpersonal and communication skills; attention to detail

Certification and Licensing
Not required, but can strengthen résumé

Working Conditions
Office environment

Salary Range
Median pay of $51,470 in 2015

Number of Jobs
About 766,900 as of 2014

Future Job Outlook
Projected growth of 12 percent through 2024

These professionals handle calls for help related to log-in problems, operating system glitches, software issues, and much more. They may help users over the phone, via e-mail, or with an in-person visit. They also often educate computer users on how to properly use software and hardware.

Some computer support specialists—called computer network support specialists—provide support for an organization's information technology (IT) employees. They test and evaluate network systems, including local area networks, wide area networks, and Internet systems. They also perform regular maintenance to keep all network components working properly, including helping back up files on the network. When a network problem occurs, these specialists help IT employees troubleshoot the problem. Resolving problems quickly is critical because networks and systems are essential to organizations' operations. Without properly functioning networks and systems, employee work can grind to a halt.

Other support specialists—called computer user support specialists—provide technical help for non-IT users. They talk to users and ask questions to identify the problem. Then they walk users through the steps needed to fix the problem. While many problems can be resolved over the phone or via e-mail, some issues require an in-person visit from the support specialist. In some cases these specialists may set up equipment for users or perform minor repairs. They may also train users to use new hardware or software, such as how to log in to a new customer tracking system or sync their devices. Some computer user support specialists also prepare information for an organization's users about common problems and solutions that many users have faced.

Felicia Thomas is a senior information systems desktop support specialist at the UTMB Health Angleton Danbury Campus Hospital in Angleton, Texas. She helps users all over the hospital with a variety of technology problems, from those that involve phones and videoconferencing to televisions and network wiring. "We touch everything in the hospital—even the cafeteria cash registers," says Thomas in a 2015 interview posted on the UTMB website. "Most people don't realize the magnitude of what we do." Each day Thomas gathers service requests from employees and decides which ones she will tackle first. Problems that are occurring in high-priority areas such as the emergency department or the operating room jump to the top of her list. In a typical day she sets up new employees on the computer network, helps with log-in problems, repairs mobile computers, and installs new software. Thomas says the best part about her job is being able to help others at the hospital. "I love this field, because I love the human interaction," she says.

How Do You Become a Computer Support Specialist?

Education

Education requirements for this position vary by job and industry. Most jobs require applicants to have solid computer skills, but a bachelor's degree is not always required. In some cases applicants who have an associate's degree or who have taken computer-related classes will be hired for the position. Students should take courses such as computer hardware, software, operating systems, networks, and diagnostics. They should also learn Windows and Mac operating systems and servers and Cisco and Microsoft products, all of which are commonly used. In some cases employers may provide on-the-job training for entry-level support specialists. Some employers prefer candidates who have a bachelor's degree in a computer-related field. For example, large software companies that provide support to companies that buy their products often want support specialists to have a bachelor's degree. Jobs that are highly technical are also more likely to require a bachelor's degree in a computer-related field.

Certification and Licensing

Although computer support specialists do not need any specific certifications or licenses to do their work, some get additional training and/ or earn a certification offered by a vendor or a third-party program. This additional work demonstrates that individuals are committed to learning more and updating their skills. Some organizations may require support specialists to earn certifications in the products and hardware that the organization uses. Some common certifications include CompTIA A+ Technician, CompTIA Network+, and Microsoft product-level certifications. To become certified, a candidate must pass an exam or series of exams.

Volunteer Work and Internships

Students interested in this field might consider doing an internship to improve their chances of landing a full-time job. While pursuing an associate's degree in computer IT at Daytona State College, Jennifer Marshall also interned at the IT service desk at the International Speedway Corporation. "I take turns with covering the phones and emails," she said in an interview posted on the Daytona State College website. "I'm learning something new every day with the type of environment we support." Marshall also used her internship to get experience doing computer network support. "I had the opportunity to work with the networking team on a few small projects," she says. "I'm now assisting them with small tasks, which will make me a better candidate for when a position does open up."

Even without an internship, hands-on experience in a related field can be beneficial. Working at a help desk or in call-center support can help workers get experience solving technical problems for users, such as log-in issues, connectivity difficulties, and other issues with computer hardware and software. This experience, along with a degree and certification, may help a candidate land a job with a higher salary and more responsibility.

Skills and Personality

Successful computer support specialists have a good mix of technical, interpersonal, and communication skills. They must be able to solve a wide variety of computer and software issues. They must be intimately familiar with hardware and software, log-in systems, e-mail applications, and networks. In addition, they must be able to assess a problem and come up with a solution to fix it. At the same time, they must be able to listen well and deal with people who are frustrated with technology.

Computer support specialists spend a large part of their time dealing with people on the phone, over e-mail, via computer chat, or through in-person meetings. Therefore, it is critical that they be able to communicate clearly and effectively. In order to correctly identify the problem a user is having with his or her computer or software, specialists must be able to ask users the right questions and listen closely to their answers. Then they need to give clear, step-by-step instructions to fix the problem. Specialists who resolve problems via e-mail should be able to write very clearly.

On the Job

Employers and Working Conditions

Computer support specialists work in many industries, such as IT, education, finance, health care, and telecommunications. According to the Bureau of Labor Statistics (BLS), there were approximately 766,900 computer support specialists working in 2014. Some work for support service firms that contract with businesses and consumers. Others work for organizations in IT education, finance, health care, and telecommunications.

Many computer support specialists work in an office environment. Some work for large software companies or support-services firms. Others, particularly help-desk technicians, work in call centers or from home. Some specialists may have to travel to a client's office to fix a problem. Most computer support specialists work full time; however, many do not work typical nine-to-five hours. Because computer support is needed twenty-four hours a day, many specialists work evening and weekend hours, with some working overnight shifts.

Earnings

According to the BLS, as of May 2015 the median annual pay for computer support specialists was $51,470. Wages ranged by position and industry from less than $28,990 to more than $106,310 in 2014. Computer network support specialists generally earned more, with a median annual wage of $62,250 in May 2015, compared to a median annual wage of $48,620 for computer user support specialists.

Specialists typically receive other benefits, which can amount to thousands of dollars. These vary but can include paid vacation and sick leave, bonuses, medical and dental insurance, education benefits and tuition reimbursement, retirement benefits, and life insurance.

Opportunities for Advancement

Many computer support specialists can advance to higher-level positions in the IT department. Some advance to become network and computer systems administrators. Others become software developers. Some support specialists are promoted to manager positions, where they are responsible for overseeing a team of specialists. Those who have additional training, such as certifications or a bachelor's degree, may be more likely to advance.

What Is the Future Outlook for Computer Support Specialists?

The job outlook for computer support specialists is very good. According to the BLS's *Occupational Outlook Handbook*, computer support specialist jobs are projected to grow 12 percent from 2014 to 2024. This growth rate is faster than the average rate for all occupations.

As more organizations upgrade their computer equipment, software, and other technology, they will need knowledgeable support specialists to assist users. Specialists will need to install and repair increasingly complex equipment and software. Smaller organizations that do not have dedicated IT departments will need to contract with consulting companies for IT support, which will open many support specialist positions at these firms. The increasing use of technology in the health care industry is also expected to grow the need for computer support specialists.

Some of the growth in this career may be slowed by the use of cloud computing, which will allow support specialists to do their jobs more effectively and productively, and in turn reduce the number of employees needed to perform the same amount of work. In addition, lower-level jobs, such as call center support, are often sent overseas to countries with lower wages. However, some organizations are choosing to move these jobs to lower-cost areas of the United States instead of foreign countries. Some companies are choosing to move the jobs back because of rising labor costs overseas, while others found their customers were unhappy with the service from overseas call centers.

Find Out More

Association for Computing Machinery
2 Penn Plaza, Suite 701
New York, NY 10121
website: www.acm.org

This organization provides resources such as publications, conferences, and career resources for IT professionals, including computer support specialists. It has members worldwide and encourages networking and sharing of information to strengthen the profession and industry.

Association of Information Technology Professionals (AITP)
1120 Route 73, Ste. 200
Mount Laurel, NJ 08054
website: www.aitp.org

The AITP works to advance the information technology profession through professional development, education, and national policies. It features webinars, conferences, awards for professionals and students, a career center with a jobs board, and networking options that are of interest for computer support specialists. It has chapters for professionals and students across the United States.

CompTIA
3500 Lacey Rd., Suite 100
Downers Grove, IL 60515
website: www.comptia.org

CompTIA provides many IT certifications and education resources for IT professionals, including computer support specialists. The organization also advocates for the IT industry at the local, state, and federal government levels.

IEEE Computer Society
3 Park Ave., 17th Floor
New York, NY 10016
website: www.ieee.org

The IEEE Computer Society is the world's largest professional organization for advancing technology and engineering globally. It provides many publications, conferences, technology standards, and professional and educational activities that are useful for computer support specialists.

Interview with a Software Developer

Cathy Holmes is a principal program manager for the SAS Institute, a software company that specializes in statistical analysis software, in Maryland. She works in a department that sells software to the US government. She has worked for SAS for sixteen years, first as a software developer. She advanced to a technical lead, team lead, and project manager before working in her current position. She answered questions about her career by e-mail.

Q: Why did you decide to work in this career?
A: I liked programming in high school—we had a really good department and some really engaging teachers. I liked the logic of writing programs—the program either worked or didn't, and you had to figure out how to fix it. I was good in Math and Science subjects. When I got to college I was torn between Physics and Computer Science majors, and Computers seems to be easier for me.

Q: Can you describe your typical workday?
A: Right now I coordinate a lot of projects and make sure they run smoothly. I have to send emails and make a lot of calls to make sure the tasks are on time, and resolve any problems that may come up. My biggest challenge is scheduling everyone—our team is in very high demand!

Q: What do you like most about your job?
A: I like my job because I work across so many organizations in our company. I feel like I have a lot of impact over the programs here at SAS and that means we have happy customers! Ultimately, our customer is the U.S. Government. We work with groups such as the Social Security Administration or Center for Medicare/Medicaid

Services and help identify people that are committing fraud against these agencies. That means we save the organizations lots of money.

Q: What do you like least about your job?

A: If our software isn't working right, we have unhappy customers and we have to figure out a way to solve the problem. That can be very stressful!

Q: What personal qualities do you find most valuable for this type of work?

A: Tenacity, creativity, communication skills, and teamwork. Software can be very complex and hard to debug. It takes patience and tenacity to work through the problems and get to a resolution. In addition, there are many ways to make software work—you get to create your own style and figure out the best way to make things happen. Also, communication skills are important. A lot of people think that writing software means you sit at your desk and don't talk to anyone. Not true. It requires a lot of communication with your development team, managers, customers, and stakeholders. Being able to communicate well is extremely important! Finally, this is not a solo career. You have to depend on your team in order to put out the best product, and they have to be able to depend on you.

Q: What advice do you have for students who might be interested in this career?

A: The world is in need of so many computer scientists and software engineers—it is a great, exciting field to be in. Just remember there are a lot of different options for you—anything from software development to network administration to system administration, and that could lead to project/program management and presales engineering. There will always be job options for these skills!

Q: What are the benefits of an internship for students? What advice do you have for someone considering doing one?

A: My advice is to do it! I did a year-long internship with the Department of Defense while in college. In college, my classes focused on the theory of computer science, and I was getting burned out on it. Doing my internship made me see how to apply what I was learning in real life—and it made me very excited about my future. Chances are the internship will be paid, so that's a bonus. Also, you have experience when you are done, which is more than most college graduates, so you have a better chance of getting a job.

Other Jobs in Computer Science

Application analyst
Artificial intelligence quality
  engineer
Business continuity analyst
Business intelligence analyst
Computer programmer
Computer software trainer
Data analyst
Data architect
Data modeler
Digital copywriter
E-commerce developer
Games developer
Information systems manager
Information technology (IT)
  auditor
IT consultant
IT sales professional
IT trainer
Mobile applications developer
Multimedia programmer

Network architect
Network engineer
Pay-per-click specialist
Portal administrator
Product manager
Quality assurance associate/
  analyst
Search engine optimization
  specialist
Social media manager
Software quality assurance tester
Software tester
Systems analyst
Systems developer
Technical writer
Telecommunications expert
User experience analyst
User experience designer
Web designer
Wireless engineer

Editor's note: The US Department of Labor's Bureau of Labor Statistics provides information about hundreds of occupations. The agency's *Occupational Outlook Handbook* describes what these jobs entail, the work environment, education and skill requirements, pay, future outlook, and more. The *Occupational Outlook Handbook* may be accessed online at www.bls.gov/ooh.

Index

Reed, John, 13
Ren, Yang, 51

Sabolcik, Ross, 29
Sandhu, Simran, 28
SANS Institute, 63
software developer, **11**
  advancement opportunities, 15
  certification/licensing, 10, 13
  educational requirements, 10, 12
  employers of, 14
  future job outlook for, 10, 16
  information resources, 16–17
  interview with, 71–73
  number of jobs for, 10
  role of, 10–12
  salary/earnings, 10
  skills/personal qualities, 10, 14
  volunteer work/internships, 13
  working conditions, 10, 14–15

Thomas, Felicia, 65–66
Totaljobs, 12

2015 Cost of Cyber Crime
  (Ponemon Institute), 16, 56

U.S. News & World Report
  (magazine), 28, 29, 38, 43, 64

Webb, Geoff, 58
web developer
  advancement opportunities,
    46–47
  certification/licensing, 42, 44
  educational requirements, 42,
    44
  employers of, 46
  future job outlook for, 42, 47
  information resources, 48
  number of jobs for, 42
  role of, 42–43
  salary/earnings, 42, 46
  skills/personal qualities, 42, 45
  volunteer work/internships, 45
  working conditions, 42, 46
Web Professionals, 48
Wilson, Jessica, 60–61

Picture Credits

About the Author

Carla Mooney is the author of many books for young adults and children. She lives in Pittsburgh, Pennsylvania, with her husband and three children.